F-WORDS

By the same author:

Cavorting with time (chapbook, 2018)

F-WORDS

JACQUI MALINS

RECENT
WORK
PRESS

F-words
Recent Work Press
Canberra, Australia

Copyright © Jacqui Malins, 2021

ISBN: 9780645009019 (paperback)

 A catalogue record for this
book is available from the
National Library of Australia

Cover image: © Jacqui Malins, 2021
Cover design: Recent Work Press
Set by Recent Work Press

recentworkpress.com

MD

*To Leonie, Peter, Jenny, Gillian and David—
with thanks for your love, encouragement, many
varieties of support and for some excellent material.*

Contents

FABLES

Birth to stones

She gives birth to stones
round, as if
they were grinding away in there
for eons
into ovals,
all edges worn
solid to the core.
They arrive in a gush of seawater
without blood or gore.

First soft grey or fawn
then ruddy with iron
traced with veins of golden sulphur
grained with flecks of copper ore.
One is onyx
another snowy quartz.
When they leave her body
they lose their warmth.
She runs her palms over
curved surfaces, smooth
or coarse. They will not hatch
and do not grow
but they endure.

She loves her mineral children
but it becomes a problem
at the office. She is fecund
and you only need so many
oversized paperweights.
She can't explain herself
share her uncanny maternity
nor answer for paternity.

There is no man, no other woman
no kneeling angel in this vignette
and yet—
she concludes the earth itself
has entered her.

When her employer asks her to leave
she needs a trolley, but she is ready
to go, wants to get off the folly
of nylon carpet, to wear bare feet
caress the earth her lover skin to skin.
She tenderly fills her small garden
with rockery, when no more stones will fit
goes wandering. Prefers unpaved trails
so her communion is not broken
by shields of bitumen. Immune to mockery
she finds niches, hollows that cup the contours
of her stone babies, leaves them there
safe in the care of their other parent.

When she dawdles she leaves meandering riverbeds.
When she runs, they are few and far between
like glacial erratics. So as not to consume
her own bones in geological process
she sips at silt, grinds gravel between shrinking molars
knows she alone must replenish herself
or become a monster like the ancestor
who turned others to stone.

In time, she is a toothless crone.
Stands on the seashore cradling
a rock crystal like a hailstone
the size of a brick. She can see
through it to her interlocked fingers

read the story in the thick creases
that mark her palms. She comes undone
cannot abandon this one.
She holds it close and dives.

It pulls her down

down

to be reborn in a gush
of seawater.

How to silver a mirror

get 1 gram each
of silver nitrate and sodium hydroxide
dissolve each in water separately
mix the two solutions
a black precipitate of silver oxide will form
add ammonia until the precipitate redissolves completely
add 4 grams of sugar and stir until it too is dissolved
pour the solution onto the back of your mirror glass
heat gently but do not boil
when this liquid turns the colour of cream
your mirror is finished.

turn it over
look in.
this is a safety mirror—not because it won't shatter
because the light reflected from your face travels
only a few microns from the surface of the glass
to the silvered reverse
before bouncing back
to your gaze.

the original mirror—a still pond or puddle
resembles the one that you silvered but more dangerous
not because the image wavers
not the risks of Narcissus or the beat-up jealousies of evil queens
not the prat-fall slapstick of falling in with a splash—an older animism
interference by objects in the soul of matter.

not all light returns direct from still water
some dives down to rebound off submerged objects
rocks—fish—water weeds—frogs—beer bottles—condensed-milk cans
shopping trollies—discarded murder weapons—submarine cables
buzzing

sunk ships—mermaids—sea monsters—
bones dropped by thieving dogs
drowned bodies.

light reflected from your face might strike any of these
any of these might imbue your refracted image
before it swims back up
to merge again with your reflection
however tranquil the surface

The bird bath

I wanted to fly so I drank the water from the bird bath
choked down slime, wrigglers, rotting leaves.
My dose of easy suffering, my magic potion.
Not even a real bird bath, just an old bowl
left out in the rain and the cold
but I had seen the wrens dunking and fluttering
thornbills and silvereyes scattering drops.
It was surely infused with essence of bird:
feathery lightness, hollow-boned-ness
bright eyed-ness and the quick snap of wings.

I wanted to fly so I drank the water from the bird bath
waited for metamorphosis, the quick snap of wings.
Sprouting feathers tingled my fingertips
the pull of pinions punctured shoulder blades.
I stroked the down that sprang from my round belly
sharpened my toenails with an emery board.
My bones lost their marrow and, lighter
I prepared to let go my hold on the ground.
I could sense my transformation from lead
into air but no one else could see this alchemy.

I wanted to fly so I drank the water from the bird bath
but no one else could see this alchemy.
The weight of expectation pressed me back
against the ground. Terrestrial, desperate
I tipped the bird bath over my head
baptised myself with what was left
stood dripping slime, wiping my eyes.
With that I vanished from polite society
into the realm of madness that can't be looked at
in case it is catching.

I wanted to fly so I drank the water from the bird bath.
Madness was no catapult into avian flight
just a sodden cloak of invisibility.
I could not be seen but could be heard so I sang
and like the bird I wanted to be I poured myself out
through imagined beak, unafraid to speak.
When the magic failed and I looked down and saw my new feathers
were the emperor's own, I crept off to hide in the internest
that basket maze of dens and eyries
to rest and preen my nakedness.

I wanted to fly so I drank the water from the bird bath
and crept off to preen my nakedness in the deep pockets of the internest
woven of twigs and stems of grass with possum fur to nestle in
a place to keep thoughts warm until they hatched
cracked the shell containing them.
Moods wicked along interwoven strands like rising damp
seeping dye, the stormy charge that arcs between clouds.
There I joined a restless flock scratching, rustling, brooding
sometimes strapping spurs to scaly ankles
to fight amidst squawking crowds.

I wanted to fly so I drank the water from the bird bath
but wise old birds of that flock taught me
more useful skills than choking down dank water
and rotting leaves—the correct use and shedding
of an egg-tooth, how to hold up your downy hatchling head
pectoral exercise in preparation for flight, how to stick a landing
to stretch the wings I hoped were there
to push against air.

I jumped.

Go wolf

i go wolf   let pelt flourish   tendrils
finger the air   antennae
for super-sensory perception   feel
water moving by the molecule subtle
stirring   of nitrogen and carbon
dioxide in the draft   my lovers
wander weedy thickets hunt scented
scrub for soft centre   Samson's
femme antithesis i shear hair   bare
l u p i n e   h e a d   f e e l s   f e a r s o m e
                              my sole predators
humans and bears   i shy
from hostile eyes   leave wolfishness
behind awhile   go back
into ladylike disguise   at least below
the knees   look down   at wolf limbs
dressed in baby skin   tender as
pinkie mice   fed   to captive reptiles

                              go wolf
                              again

The barrel

after Aldous Harding

a plucked wire figure repeats
plectrum engine propelling
perpetual motion
arpeggio
follow ivory chimes through
the burrow to where she
waits, oscillates in
puritan dress
jacked-up sneakers, singular maiden
gleaming to see you
she feels your
love
sings silver-suede of ferrets and
eggs, dares you to get
her metaphors
know
what she means, unconsummated
key-change teases, shape shifts
the blue-faced crone is
dancing
the child voice sings askew
of time and tune
the music
stops

hold   the   gap   between   lashes

melodic engine
kicks back into motion
she feels time is up, cuts a caper
back away, back out of
the barrel

She lets us go

Gravel stirs, dust and rubbish gyre a sudden storm
outdoor furniture not anchored scuffles
a dance with wheelie bins and pot plants
waves start to break—up—and globs of water spin
splash sunbakers who drift on magic carpet towels
parked cars shift and shuffle as if in a flood
abandoned trolleys levitate, flying dogs howl
trucks grinding uphill strike the crest
sail their tangent uninterrupted

Don't just drift away!
Grab what you can –
fence, tree, lightpole
drag yourself arm over arm
to a bolthole. Seal the doors
and windows fast
while the air lasts

We saw her as mother
thought she would nurture us
whatever hot air we blew
tantrums we threw
but she was our lover
We didn't wake up—
now it's a break up
She knew life before us
she will recover

She made excuses for our abuses
to Venus, her confidante
kept her secrets from Mercury,
'cause he'd gossip to the whole galaxy
hid her scars from Mars
who's started wars for less

Resigned, she sighs
blows us a kiss goodbye
releases the intimate embrace
of her gravity
Hold on   if you can
or   float   into   space

When her grieving is done
she will shrug her gravitational cloak
back over mountain shoulders
ready to be attractive once more.

Tiny subterranean creatures might remain
to kick off evolution once again. She will
chalk the anthropocene up to experience
have better taste in lovers next time around.

FAMILY

Word glutton

I gobble words
stuff them into eyes and ears
until my head is overfull
suffer verbal indigestion
later, verbal diarrhoea.

I started young.
As soon as I could read
I would sneak extra words
when no-one was watching.

No shoplifting nail varnish or lipgloss
my childhood vices age-inappropriate literature
at the municipal library
and reading in the bathroom
an illicit act indeed
in a house with four children
and one toilet. When that was stopped
I resorted to copy on the back of
artificially fragrant aerosol cans like
a smoker sucking on a half-smoked
discarded, retrieved and reignited butt.

At breakfast, the back of cereal packets
lunch, the school library
dinner, excusing myself at the first opportunity
my book so much more compelling
than chops and mashed potato
or Mum's savoury mince.

No sleep before the last page
...but there's always another book.

I'm still not one to stop and smell the proses.
I snort lines of text like lines of coke
at the expense of sleep
engulf sentences and paragraphs whole
barely remembered.

How does a word glutton read poetry
which needs savour?
To linger over the flavour of sounds and syllables?
When each word must be sniffed delicately
held up to the light
swirled around my mouth
over my tongue and lips?

Poetry is a drag—
not to get me down, but
like the tethers I've seen swimmers tow
to build their strength
—to slow me down enough to give these words
the mastication they deserve.
Chew them properly
before here
I spit them out

Ode to savoury mince

Mum's savoury mince, Sunday night special, no secret recipe.
Take a tight budget, no love of cooking, four kids
electric frying pan, element not quite up to the job
(you don't want to brown your mince, you want to grey it)
Push around half a kilo of flesh and fat until it sweats.
Prod it with an egg-lifter to break it up.
Toss in a bag of frozen mixed veg
(they're just as healthy, Rosemary Stanton said)
Add a packet of French onion soup mix
for aroma more than flavour
(tomorrow it will scent your skin)
Thicken with cornflour lumps and serve
over two slices of brown toast with margarine.
That's seventies anglo convenience cuisine, though
the wog kids' mums would not have called it food.
It wasn't all bad. I cook her gingernuts and pavlova.
Crave, then regret, her spaghetti (nothing an Italian would own)
baked with Rosella tomato sauce and grated Kraft cheddar.
Harbour nostalgia for 'ambrosia': sherry-soused marshmallows
with canned pineapple and mandarin, desiccated coconut, sour cream.
But O savoury mince! it contained her grit in its consistency,
persistence in the lingering odour of French onion soup
nurture in the way the mince and gravy
enfolded the toast in warm embrace.

Labour

Stop-motion memory
like super-eight
accelerates
our old backyard

bare block erupts brick box
grass spills, saplings spear
shrubbery boils over
retention walls crawl

cement hems rocks
backfilled slopes tilt up
extensions sprout out
like extra limbs

freeze an early frame

zoom in

I hold the hose while Dad mixes concrete
in the chipped wheelbarrow, my eyes graze its rim
sweat and water trickle while the mattock
grates a rhythm of gravel on metal

When they left that house I didn't blink
now the years he carted soil, stone, brick
press heavy. Like any work that lasts
his labour is passed to someone else

Over the back fence

Working at a wildlife park
the neighbour's daughter
brought home a dingo pup.
Hidden by grey palings
glimpsed through cracks
(except for one leap to brief freedom)
the golden not-dog grew as we grew.
We could roam to find our kind
it could not. Alone all day it called
casting for kin with its ululating cry.
Determined to re-enter the world
with more credentials than when
she left to bear us, my Mother bent
over her desk. The penetrating song
persists too, one more reason
to pass her test.

My father's body

My father's body would be laid out on the operating table, face pale and distorted by tubes, pipes, masks stuck on with tape, eyes closed, and the machines doing his breathing, pumping his blood for him, mind asleep and body beyond pain, paralysed as the scalpel slices into the crêpey skin and then the bone and cartilage of his ribcage, he isn't a man who carries much fat. Maybe a saw would be involved next, spreaders to splay the ribcage like a bone basket cupping lungs and heart. The lungs lie still, an instant of rest, of risk, while the scalpel goes further, into the heart itself, allowing probes and cameras into the valves to seek the infection they have not been able to see from outside but know is there. Golden staph is stealthy, cocoons into capsules beyond the reach of immune system infantry, so they probe, peer, cut, peel, find a nest, a hive of gilded single-celled invaders. A bacterium isn't even a whole cell, no nucleus, but even so they have colonised his heart, made it home and hearth, must now be evicted, cut out, sluiced. The valve, which keeps the blood going in one direction around lungs and brain and body, not sloshing back and forth, is replaced with one taken from the heart of a pig, which at least has died for a purpose more noble than pork chops or sausages, though the pig did not realise this even though they are intelligent animals. When the surgeon is satisfied that he has washed this muscular pump clean of infection, left it with enough operational parts to do its job in part, he works backwards, mops up, makes sure nothing from outside is left inside except for the pig's valve, which to an inexperienced eye would look indistinguishable from the man's own tissue. He joins, stitches, works up through the layers, pressing together the bone and cartilage until he is stitching up the skin, this will leave one visible scar to be joined by others when they implant a machine to tell his heart when to stop fidgeting or shivering. Now the stitching is finished, the drugs are switched, tape peeled away, tubes slipped out. My father's eyes open, he has seen none of this, but his voice, altered by the pressure of tubes, tells us he is changed.

Wizard of Whitebridge

My mother's father, tall, a flourish of white hair
and bizarre repertoire of snake oil and coffee enemas.
Vibrating massage table, appliances for stretching the spine
chiropractic wall charts, acupuncture needles.
Two grey vinyl lounge chairs his waiting room, where my sister and I
would swing our legs and leaf through People magazines
while he saw patients who came looking for cures
remedies and the laying-on of hands.
They found them too—they told us at his funeral.

Behind the curtained consulting rooms
a workshop scented with oil, concrete
liniment, shelves to the ceiling stacked
with jars and margarine containers
tin cans filled with nails and nuts and bolts
bits and pieces for clever tinkering.
Metal lathe a shrine to which he sacrificed
the tip of one finger. Engineer of
model trains big enough to ride.
Behind, again, a contained wasteland
of long grass, one gigantic aloe vera
a low corrugated iron lean-to.
He had to crawl in.
I only ever saw him haul out timber
but the big boys next door told me
he used it to imprison children.

He died four years after being struck.
Strove against the stroke for two
then worked to finish its job with too much strength
too little dexterity to go quickly.

They cleared out his shed, found a coffin.
Home-made. Fortunately empty. Built, they surmised
to prove how outrageous the price of undertakers.
He was already cremated.

The guides

I don't believe in an afterlife, but if I did, and
died today, who would appear to be my guides?

My fortunate family has so far expired
in the expected order. The only dead
I know were robust adults when I was
a child, then fragile and fading.
My grandmothers were the last to go.

Grandmother Lorna arrives stylish, taste
for white fake fur and peacock blue enduring.
She still sets her thin hair in foam curlers
each night, coaxing its fawn floss into a
French roll each morning, serves exotic food
like cheese soup with croutons, thrives on
drama, intrigue and her sense of persecution.

Grandmother Dorothy is taking longer
because she's been up a stepladder with
the vacuum cleaner. Rewound to back
before the heart attack she survived, she
is smoking, sipping a glass of ale, her steel-grey
set a weekly affair at the hairdresser. Discipline,
housekeeping and humour all keen and harsh.

Or would they be as I saw them last? Would I
have to guide them, freshly dead myself?

Lorna is bedridden but as happy as I ever saw,
all histrionics and words lost in a mist of dementia.
She smiles in placid delight, croons a wordless melody.

Dot, brittle-boned and tiny, clearer of mind,
is less sharp of tongue but still querulous,
riding gunshot as I drive her out to lunch,
joking when I take a wrong turn,
Don't lose me! Don't lose me!

Downhill run

I set a good example,
stop us at crossroads
look both ways before
we bolt again, half-racing-
half-keeping-pace. Her blunt
cut hair swings straight as a
plumb along her chin (like her
mother's (my sister's) did).
On the freeway overpass
we stop to feel the concrete
shudder through our feet
in its rubber-jointed cradle
as trucks rush underneath.
Our goal the glowing colonial
bungalow festooned with iron lace
and LEDs, attracting moths and a
minor traffic jam. Admire the
moulded plastic nativity, airbrushed
and lit from inside, the motorised
santa ho-ho-hoing, meccano reindeer
nodding to crop the grass. With wires
and frames hidden by the glare of their
illumination, even the flourescent-tube
candy-canes are magic. We pose for selfies
while her parents and dusk catch us up.
Back on the bridge a tarmacadam of bats
pours across the last sunglow, a parallel arc
of dark clawed leather mirroring the flight of
headlights below. To find fruit they flee
their traffic island of gum trees draped in
dust-sheets of lantana and morning glory,
purple flowers folded for the night.

FARAWAY

Budget travel

We hiked monolithic valleys in clay-oven heat
skirted elegant troglodyte dwellings nestled
into the brow of squinting cliffs.
Backpacking in Cappadocia—
every second Aussie was doing it that year.

Peering into chapels painted by Byzantine hermits
pockmarked by vandals, sweat seeping
from elbow creases
we made our final ascent
to Club Med Uçhisar.

Cheapskates, we wouldn't stay but scraped up
entry to the swimming pool which included
the use of towels much cleaner than ours
plus two Efes pilsners to swig on the terrazzo
alongside the other half.

I waded in, wallowed in cool until a shock
bombardment—was I target or collateral?
A squadron of swifts dived in on herringbone trajectories
each bird swiftly dipping a sip on the wing
wheeling to dip again.

Submerged, eyes at the waterline, I saw the formation
split and splice, braid threads of light
beaks prick dimples in water's skin
set a net of intersecting ripples to snare me.
Then they strafed me with delight.

Away

It was the longest I had been away
from the familiar. Hadn't got
the hang of Spanish—it's like Italian,
they said, but my ears couldn't
untangle it. I sat in a Madrid cafe
with cortado, bollos, feet
overheating in new plush-lined
winter boots I was lucky to find—
I was too big for nearly everything.
Balanced on a bentwood chair
I rocked between returning to
eucalyptus air and travelling on.

Crash. Man on the floor.
Heart attack? Writhing, twitching.
Not fitting—fully present
eyes aware, bulging under brows
lumped like knuckles, face red and wet
with sweat as he stared over the rim
of existence. So close to me
to leave, I would have to
step over him. People shouted
things I couldn't comprehend.
I didn't know or love this man
but grieved that he brought death
closer to me than home. Face red and wet
with shameful tears I couldn't stem,
I waited. Looked out at wire skeletons
of daytime Christmas lights. Paramedics
arrived on foot, the only way through
antique streets. They treated him,
carried him away. I wouldn't know
his fate. I wiped my face, paid
stepped back out into the day.

The border

As far from the ocean as you could go
and still be in Portugal, we could see wind
farm blades turning lazily in Spain. We
headed out from our lodging to hike
argued about our direction. Coming from
an island nation we didn't want to stumble
into the wrong country by accident.
Forests. Mountains. Farmland. A village
restaurant, where we ordered chicken
and wine by waving our hands. Heading
back up the mountain, thirsty from wine
and chicken, we ran out of water, argued
about our direction, didn't want to stumble
into the wrong country by accident.
Found a spring, found our way. Footsore
exhausted, we ordered beer, bread and cheese
by waving our hands. The woman at the bar
gave us raspberry jam. We contemplated
its crimson, talked by waving our hands
stopped arguing about our direction
stumbled into different countries.

View from Zeta Leporis

I
fill
my
lungs
push off
from this
rock kick out
into air   freed
from gravity's cling
gain speed swoop past
the moon   jupiter   cool
as I zoom further from our sun
pass stars   travel far fast   the speed
of poetry   defying   special relativity
limitless   source of energy   slow   float alone   near

Zeta Leporis   sixth star   in the constellation
of   the   hare   a   solitary animal   Zeta Leporis
arrayed in   dazzling   asteroid   belt

I spin   peer back at point of light that is our sun   squint at a
speck on that bright diminutive disk   earth's shadow I get a fix
it is November there, seventy-point-five light-years away   ago
Scott Street   toddler Mum slides down her mother's knees
she and her brother play that the white lambskin rug is snow
my gaze swivels fraction of a degree earth-south to Kerang
where five-year-old Dad trots across the triangular yard
on duckboards to his sleepout past peach trees past
the laundry with its bricked-in copper its concrete
trough and water tank   the past is another
planet   I know I must go back   by the
time I crash land these children will have
moved   met   married   conceived
birthed me   my sisters   my brother
we grow   now middle-aged   so
strange   feel the same I play
with time with space but
cannot stay I close my
eyes into cold steel
of wind speed
free fall feel
my way
down
into
now

Honeybilla Moon Quartet

Honeybilla 1969

latticed ear
searches the sky
not for music of the spheres
but voices, visions, vital signs
of little gods
touched by the heavens
bowl catches invisible signal
giant spool draws down
the fragile S-band thread
bridges gap between
ground and goddess
tethers the Eagle
stitches a TV memento
where were you, when...?

Moon 1969

small step
corporeal contact
humility, hubris
celestial body now substance
object in our minds
marks made and left
dust etched
boots on the moon's face
footprints our fingerprint
until we return
or eternity
whichever comes first

Moon 2019

human touch lingers
persistent
visible to machine eyes
sidereal scans snag shadows
strangely symmetrical
amongst lunar acne
landing section—launch pad
our fragile trash lies there
still
incorruptible relics
left to
not rot

Honeybilla 2019

razed
dismembered by astronomers
concrete slabs daubed with birds' deposits
asphalt eaten by weeds and weather
memorialised with interpretive signs
eucalypts encroach
this old footprint will fade
long before the boot-marks
on the face of
moon

The Federal

As I pass Lake George and pull up the next rise, I have the feeling I feel every time I do this trip, that I am almost home, and then I realise there is another half hour of rolling hills, farmland and bits of bush, that may, depending on the season and the year, be bleached beige or prickling green and chartreuse or dotted with golden wattle-puffs, and even though the green of the coast was home for so long, this paler grittier landscape is now the familiar and I feel myself relaxing as I pass well-known turn-offs and signs and finally run over the last hill before the suburbs begin to see Black Mountain Tower poised like a needle against the last light on the western ridge and lights of Gungahlin are spread out to my right and they remind me of the slide down Mount Ousley on the drive back to Wollongong after visiting my grandparents as a child when the lights would be spread in a ribbon below the cliffs. The tip of the tower disappears below the treetops and I come up to the first of two turns that could take me to my own street and lane and garage and back door, but this time I am on a longer journey, so I keep on due south, alongside the Starlight Apartments on the highway, past the showground and exhibition pavilions and strike the junction with the light rail, the red carriages running along what was once a tree-lined median, the replacement trees are at least surviving, mostly, and I can see the people inside the carriage as we run along in parallel, me in my red hatchback and them inside the lighted capsule, we journey strangely together until the next intersection and I have to stop and wait while it runs ahead of me to the terminus, where I overtake it again among the corridors and gorges of office buildings and apartment blocks and then I chicane around city hill, over the bridge, the lake, slingshot off to the left, ricochet overhead to the right like a bearing in a pinball table, and am flung south once more on the Monaro, cutting through straggling valley suburbs up the mountains, up to solitude, up to the tentative promise of snow.

Three Aprils

1.
I see the Athabasca river
frozen white, Cassiopeia's bitter glint,
a raw-boned bear scrambling up the ridge
at dawn, a pileated woodpecker's red beret
work its way percussing to the top of a
lodgepole pine. How a leaf in sunshine
on snow, each edge a warm blade, melts
a perfect tunnel, glows in its cool hole.

2.
I see my dead-skin-dust pile up
on the bedside chest, threads of mould
steal out through shower grout, stale
exhalations smudge glass, charred
crumbs accumulate in the oven's guts,
dropped leaves print tannic shadows
slow on damp cement, how anxious
scratching wears through skin to flesh.

3.
We look for Halley's comet,
join beachside crowds out late with kids
in dressing gowns, jostle for vantage
free from steelworks flare, wait for the
spectacle! Telescopes totter on segmented
legs, binoculars dangle. In peripheral vision,
the cosmic curveball faintly glimmers.
Looked at straight, it disappears.

FEELING

Dictionary

I will not climb into your dictionary
like a vaudeville magician's lovely assistant
folding herself into a box
ready to be sliced into bits that fit.
I will not join your taxonomy—
slide into the Linnaean cupboard
to line up with the other glassy-eyed
specimens for you to classify.
I ring outside the bell curve, am not normal distribution
and I can't write a prescription to save you from confusion.
You cannot match my shape to the spatters in your atlas
to figure where I fit in your jigsaw puzzle world.
I am unknown territories that I am still exploring.
I am *there be monsters*, I recognize no borders.
I will not wear your printed name tag
and I won't scratch one in texta
to make it easy for you
to find me in your lexicon.
I do not have a synonym
a pseudonym, or acronym.
My definition
is still being written
and won't be done
until I am over
and become.

Early

Chopped strips of dilute light slip through
the blinds. Not Venice. Streetlight shine
intrudes, frost filtered. Not city
flashing neon, hard-boiled crime show
detective dive. Suburban line.
Edgelands gap-toothed bite. A car stirs
birds call the sun, know it's coming.
Before it does, the stripes soften
blur. Light puddles, albumen-clear
and raw beside graffiti wall
of cockatoo noise, then thickens
congeals white. It is not yet time
for the days with a golden yolk.

Crying

I cried. Crossing the street, on the footpath
quietly in the library, loudly in my car. I cried
at how sad my crying was, and how ridiculous
there being nothing to cry about. I had
spent the night on a boat rocking violently
on two high seas: one within, one without.
With no ballast of sleep I disembarked
travelled inland for hours. Should long
have left salt water behind, but it dripped
and dripped. Better to have sprung a leak out
I guessed. A leak in could sink me, but this seeping
gentler than bailing or the bilge pump, set me
drip by drip, almost imperceptibly higher in the water.

Cassandra

I dragged Cassandra with me
so much cautious wisdom
so much extra weight.
She was drawn to the neighbourhood
by something in my temperament.
My mother gave her my exact address
inoculated me against the curse
that her prophecy would not be believed.
Sometimes I trailed her behind me
fingers tangled in a hank of her hair.
You'd think she would lose some skin that way but she
proved durable.
Other times she held me in a headlock
elbow clamped to my sternum
dry lips brushing my ear
with whispered prognostications
     like tinnitus.
I must have scratched her fingers from my throat in sleep
between mosquito bites and dreams.

     I woke buoyant on silence.

Let go a load carried long and gravity recedes.
You touch the earth lightly, on your feet or on your knees.
I didn't escape my fate just by getting out of earshot.
My civilization will crumble as foretold.
Uncivilise me, please.

Reverse archaeology

Enough excavation. No more dusting away
the matrix with squirrel hair or toothbrush.
No more peeling back the skin, picking scabs
to inspect the wound. No more vivisection.
Putty up the gaps, paper over the cracks
slap on a coat of paint in the colour of the moment.
Accrue layers, let the grit in the wind stick.
Another coat will cling to each brushstroke
and drip. Encrust with pebbles, leaves
feathers, bottle tops, beetle's wings.
Crack me open, see the growth rings.

Hold light

hold light, not tight.
don't leave pale prints from
the grip of your fingertips
let your breath touch the skin
but not your lips, let the magnetic fields
in the fine hair of your forearms engage
and propel you along parallel lines
for a while but don't converge.
Don't test the surface tension
of the epidermis, the poles
might reverse or worse
snare so the only escape is to tear.
Let the delicate meniscus suspend you
taut, just above the rim but don't
fall in. Draw into each other's wake
the space of displaced air that was
the other's volume, but do not touch.
If the final layer that envelops you is breached
you might break or awaken.

Ironmongery

Iron-clad guarantees
my grandmother's watch
my weight in gold
copper coins
tin ears
nerves of steel
all this lost
or forgotten
ironmongery drops
between collar bones
clangs like bells
against swords
swallowed in
spectacular
performance
dislocated jaw
impossible gullet
gastric acid
erases
hallmarks
stomach
muscles
crush
intricate
nuggets
cough up
walk away
lighter

Fresh

I walked home a different way today
two blocks west of my usual route.
Still air buffeted my face from unexpected directions
light refracted through shopfront glass at odd angles
glinted weirdly off street signs.
eyes of passers-by were more alive
and the traffic hummed a microtone
lower or higher – I couldn't decide.
I came to our house, which hadn't moved an inch, was sure
someone had washed the windows, the curtains were new
A familiar stranger, you assured me nothing had changed.
I didn't believe you.
Something fresh between us.

Screwtop jar

In that harbour town
in that South American bar
in our first proximity
a screwtop jar of lightning buzzed and hummed
Was that sound my gut? I had forgotten
I was hungry. Bold-faced
I looked straight through the glass
past the spark. Back in port
we sit in a pub with ships etched on the windows,
flicker in its darting light. I toss words overboard,
admire the way you catch them, throw
them back, accurate but with a different spin.
Either or, neither nor—exactly yours.
We embark on sea legs,
hold the glass out lantern-like
to find our dark. Unscrew the lid
capsize the jar.

Sky spills out

A quilt of pearled and purpled
cloud lies limp, twitching
on the drenched bed.
Mist obscures every mirror.
An exercise in gentleness.

We twist the lid back on
with our lips

One friend

I had made one friend, ok, she was eccentric, but so was I, and she was a bit bossy, but she seemed to understand the way invisible unspoken things worked better than I did, we drifted around the bitumen trying to look purposeful and not at all as if we were friendless, rudderless, in our pale blue and white checked tunics, unfashionable shoes, even uniforms can't banish fashion entirely, we were twelve, her name was Sarah, no, it was 's-ah-rah', not 's-air-rah', her father was German and that made her much more worldly, I hadn't even been on a plane but she would tell me about her trips to Germany, later I discovered she had never been, at times we talked, at times we were silent, at times we took refuge in the library, at times we would wash up on the shores of an island, a ring of blue-painted benches, blue like our tunics in honour of St-Mary-Star-of-the-Sea, my mother had observed that Catholics pronounced it 'Saint Mary's' with the hard 'ay' whereas we interlopers of protestant stock swallowed the 'ay' into 'S'nt', Snt Marys, but I was trying to speak the local language, saint, saint, and these islands had cliffs of blue-and-white-plaid-clad backs, waterfalls of long hair, black, brunette, blond, hanging gardens of ponytails and plaits, the odd snake, maybe Sah-rah's neat bob and my practical short cut left us without ropes to tie us on, no tendrils to entangle us, maybe that is why we were exposed, unmoored, the inlets between the benches were ferocious channels where you could be beaten to death on exposed social strata if you didn't get your approach just right, still, to swim too long alone in the open schoolyard meant sharks and Sah-rah and I were starting to look like waterlogged corpses rolling back and forth in the hostile tide, so we struck out for an island, squeezed in, eased between the blue benches, insinuated ourselves, thought we had made it, our disguise had held, dragged our weary bodies above the wrack to safety, but the next day we arrived with packed sandwiches in our nail-bitten hands and the circle of heads turned like fairground clowns and a spokesgirl, I don't remember who, a spokesgirl announced that SHE, that's Sah-rah, could stay, but SHE, that's me, had to go, so I went, waded bleeding back out into the asphalt sea, guts spilling from the sudden slash I sensed in my abdomen, understood the relief I recognised in Sarah's eyes as I washed away on the ebbing tide through the quadrangles and corridors, to spin with the flotsam of the wasteland whirling high school gyre

FEMINISM

The Patriarchs

that they can   hurt us   that when push
comes to shove   the ugly open secret
at the foundation   leads
                              us
               back
a map   a memorandum
cyberhaters packsinpublicplaces dailynews
words   figures   dollars   more usual tools
rational adults   so we must play nice
act all civilised   written in the mortar
is the lore that the top is their rightful place
but throw down the stones   we prise out
we're picking at the edges   of the edifice
now   let's not forget to thank these gods
as we should   so   much   magnificent
effort they have spent   for our own good
               for thinking men homo sapiens
ruling empire requires   justification
fragilityinstabilityneedforprotectivecustody
biology and medicine soon confirmed with
overwhelming evidence it's common sense!
so   science   dressed   brute force
arms not long enough
                              they picked up sticks
fists not big enough
                              picked up stones
to   fight   strike   protect
the mother of their child   bend her
to their will   make sure   she was never
their   competitor   for   anything
they were   bigger   stronger
back before   we were human

Disarming

The girl is told that she is a bomb
at nine, or ten, or thirteen or when
men want to do what they want.
The girl is told that she is a bomb.
Her girl-bomb-body explosive, she makes the
men want to do what they want.
The girl is told that she is a bomb.
Her spark of existence will light the fuse
set explosion in motion beyond their restraint.
The girl is told that she is a bomb
that makes men say things, makes men do things
makes men do things to her.
The girl is told that she is a bomb.
They gave her this power so that the men can
do what they want without consequence.
The girl is told that she is a bomb
so it's just and right that she pays the price.
Look what she made them do!
The girl wishes that she was a bomb
whose eruption's destruction for men too close
men who touch, men who are rough.

The girl is told she is not that kind of bomb.

The girl is told that she is a bomb
and must disarm and use her charm
so no-one gets hurt.

Mincing

taut unflexable
fine hide binds me on twin
pedestals protection of a sort from
cold hard nights on the tiles feints don't-mess-
with-me heights percusses my clip-clop coming
tense tendons wind slack skein calves into balls
toepads pressed like fingertips bunched
to kiss bellissima this vertiginous
perspective overrides

tip-tilted
commas

instinct attentive to
every step move like I'm looked
at look at myself in lockstep gait all weight
focused to a blunt nub each tread beating crease
between toes and ball into a squint flinch so release
feet unbind the ties embossed skin white then pink
as blood seeps in the load shared fairly
by myriad bones suspended
in jellied flesh

tarsals
bowed

Silent guest

Photographs testify to
a silent guest at all our parties
sometimes holding out
a helpful change of clothes
in the flickering
light of years of cake
candles and children multiply.
A tradition begun by oversight
we later got the ironing board out
for fun on purpose so the pictures
would be complete.

Häxan

Silent celluloid flickers witches
across my field of vision. 1922, Christiansen
looks back to the middle ages.
Malleus Maleficarum!

Which woman would not be a witch?
Massaging salve into plump or withered backs
they anoint each other with witches' ointment
bestowing with each caress the power of flight.

Now mounted on brooms, witches flicker across the screen
Don't sweep the sky clean! Flocks of women arise
alike from peasant drudgery or castle cages
with big sticks clenched between their thighs.

They don't penetrate the air – it bears them,
blowing skirts out ahead, hair forward about their faces
They have tamed the wind, broken it in!
Ecstatic, they ride it hard.

In the background the Devil frantically beats his drum,
hot as hell to see them fly.
Kissing his arse in fealty looks like a small price
for such freedom.

FLIGHT

Raven

Raven scrambles
to a wet metal landing.
Rubbery flesh thuds
under fine claw scatter
faint rain patter.
Scrapes caked meat from beak to gutter
first one side, then the other.
Shakes green-limned beard
black taffeta pleats.
Overhead too-heavy feet pound
my left ear, then
my right.
With too-human exclamation
drops off the edge
turns weight into flight.

Not Icarus

we know all about Icarus—
the father
the son
the ambition
the wax
the feathers
the soar and loft
the sun
the higher! higher!
the softening
the plummet and plunge
the splash
the dying

I am more interested
in the ways to fall
and survive.

Into Melbourne

the shadow
of our hollow dart
bumps over country clad
in crumpled blue-green
workaday plaid flannel

at dusk it drops its daks
changes for the cocktail hour
into austere black velvet
a few diamond studs
winks back at the stars

as we descend, the city
strips off starched collar
pinstripes, spiked heels
bares sunset's reflected flesh
drapes window-glass lamé
street light sequins
to vamp at the moon

Gravity speaks to Joe Kittinger

You have known me as well as anyone
who lived to tell the tale
your life—a blink
in the stare of my age
your tumbles in the tumult of my waves
barely a flutter.

You bore my pressure.

Born in the decades when humans grew restless
wanted to leave home
full, like any adolescent
of limitless (self-assessed) potential
and the silvery promise of sci-fi
these were the times!
but needing to be sure
the door was left
ajar.

So they played like Galileo, your body the cannonball
how far and fast could you fall and live?
Your mission—Excelsior – ever upwards!
(but it was always about the descent)
Excelsior 1—a tangled line and a flat spin
more than twenty times my force
then oblivion.
If I wasn't your unit of measurement, I would be humbled!
Only automation saved you.
Excelsior II—a taste of the edge of space
returned safe.
So here we are at Excelsior III – the highest step in the world.

Rise in the wake of your polyethylene bubble
float to the surface of the ocean of air
helium jellyfish drifting at the rim of the stratosphere
no edge, just a fadeout to space, where auroras play.
Suck on canned air, especially prepared
even deep sky divers get the bends.

The horizon curves below your open craft
and the truth—that the earth is a ball of dirt—is
incontrovertible
but glorious dirt! A cobalt marble with whorls of pearl
my hikaru dorodango – my shiny mud ball
formed in the grip of my discarnate fist.

The fleece of cloud is a false comforter
illusion of a soft landing.
Above, you see unconquerable void
but I feel the tug of distant cousins.
You mistake epic indifference for hostility
but are correct that the universe is indomitable
that you are a mote.

Up 20 miles, you leave the air behind
wonder if I am still there?
If you kept going, would you fall
away?
You are beyond all help but mine
only I can get you down from here.
You are right to fear.
Your suit seal has split, your right hand strains to escape
swollen like a grape in the rain
You must yield.
Stand on the edge of your gondola.

Step off
I've got you

silence   stillness   spinning.

The world turns over and over
you the hub that it tumbles around
are you a falling leaf or the centre of the universe?
I haul you down. No air, no sound
no wind whistles at the seams of your suit
no folds of fabric snap, you hang.
Look down on the crawling carpet of cloud, roll over to look back
at your balloon. It races away from you into the black
abandoning you far from anything human
you think about how alone you are

In these stretched seconds, you realise
the balloon is still, caught between my downward drag
and the skerrick of helium pressure
still pushing at its glassy onion-dome.
It is you that moves, dives back towards the world
though the thin air doesn't yet brush the cheek
of your helmet

listen to your trapped breath.

You will be lower
before I clench air in my fist
dense enough to buffet and batter
kick you into a sycamore spin, a whirligig
but you cast out—a tiny parachute
the drogue steadies you.
a sky anchor?

Not spun into darkness, you witness your own descent
the stiffening air resists your return
the volume amps up
roaring over your rough form
at a thousand kilometres per hour straight down.
My grip tightens, your speed multiplies
and at last you release your full-sized chute.
Throw these things away, they catch you with their strings
brake you before your break
slow you so you won't drive a hole through the earth's surface.

Your chute slips you nearly out of my grasp
flying machines buzz to greet you, do a waggle dance
seeking the nectar of your courage
kiss the earth hard
love the sand, salt grass and sage.

The storm speaks to Ewa Wisnierska

I watch from a distance.

I don't exist, yet, not in my final form.
I am ephemeral, ineffable
but I won't let that go to my thunderhead.

Puny featherless birds, with flimsy jellybean apparatus
sprinting across a hill to catch the rising draft
chasing one another to no destination.
And you, Ewa, do not look like the toughest in the flock
but your stance spells determination—
you are addicted! Fixated on flight.

Up here I can't blame you
I have never been cursed with weight
solidity
been netted by fences, caught within walls
I am a shapeshifter
here and there and there at once
I appear and disappear like a dream
who am I to begrudge you the hit, the high of flight
chasing ecstasy through space?

It is bright today!
The scalloped curves of cumulus could cut
but belie their true nature—moist amoebae
that engulf and disgorge you, changed.
You and your kind know my potential
your instruments have picked up hints of me beyond the horizon
but for now, swoop and glide through clear air
wind thrumming your cables, the crackle of radios
your only tether to the ground.

How far can you go?
Further?
Further!
How fast can you fly?
How high?

You see me now, crouched. I gather my parts
swallow my neighbours, pile up with each merger
insatiable
I did not come for you, Ewa
I started on this path before you were born.
In the chaos of weather I could only be predicted a moment ago
but I am of moment
and my momentum is inexorable.

Here I come, ready or not.

You are under me now. Feel my first spit and spatter
shots over your bow.
You can't see my terrible height, how I have risen like dough
while you focused on the chase.
I grow faster than I can eat, guts hollow
a vacuum, a volume that must be filled.
I gasp like a drowner
inhale you.

You ascend as if I had pinched the top of your canopy
between finger and thumb
plucked you up in one smooth lift.
My breath you ride
leave air you know behind
black out
fly blind.

In this dead zone I see
the inert object is most stable
hung like a stone
your body slows to a glacial pace
ice turns nylon parasol to providential steel
dangle in your cocoon, ragdoll limp
circling
silent.

You slow-dance inside me for an hour.
Below, I put on a show—flash, crash, hurl a bolt
strike one of your fellows
fatally.
Up here is graceful stasis
trace your circles
through my finest vapours.

Maybe I'll keep you for company?
I would have to fight gravity. Eventually she claims you.
Your circles spiral, you plunge
into violence
into breathable air
into viable warmth
into
consciousness
into
waking nightmare
into banshee wail, hail and howling descant
into numb limbs, hands rubber in their gloves.
Despite all this you cling to your grips
haul your chute to a defensive tilt
descend a demented corkscrew dropping
faster than I lifted you.

From my cold crucible you are reborn
emerge to find the earth still there!
A landscape painting waits to catch you
too hard?
Soft enough.

Ice-pummelled, gale-bruised you lie still
until your cellphone rings
tinny in frostbitten ears.
You will be saved.
You will be shocked
to learn how long you flew
intimate, insensible, inside me
Don't bother railing or blaming.
Don't thank me for your saving.

I am already gone.

Rained out.

Sea Eagle

The sea eagle
in fringed white cowboy trousers
rides the wind down,
skirting white caps,
talons out.
Rises with wriggling silver target
grasped tight,
no rope required.

FLORA & FAUNA

Hatchling

Roseate skin, bruised subcutaneous
bead of closed eye, naked body
half in/half out of its shell—can't tell
you now whether the egg was tinged
with dilute blue or lightly freckled.
I was thrilled. Found an old cake pan
in the sandpit, a cleaning rag, built
a nest. Lifted the hatchling off
the damp lawn, laid it in.

When I showed my find to Mum
she told me that it wasn't sick
but dead. That no matter how warm
I kept it, tenderly nursed it, it wouldn't
wake or heal, grow or fledge.

Yes, she was sure.

I didn't believe her, of course.
I held it in my two live hands, saw
the same quick in its pink skin.

I smuggled it into my room, tucked it
under the bed. Two days later Mum found it.
The odour of death tipped her off,
had grown overnight to fill the room while
I slept in it, oblivious.
She took the pan away, left me
a new comprehension.

If you

If you are reading this I may be dead
or alive and you have survived past
infancy, a lifeform holding your place
in the flow of time through your body's
growth, decay, autophagia, in continuous
asynchronous loops, sprouting and
shedding in mere days the lining of
the guts that stoke your fire; the rosy
surface of your cervix (if you have one);
the alveoli budding in your lungs.

If you are reading this I may be dead
or alive but every month you must be
relinquishing and recoating your eroding
skin and endometrium (if you have one),
draining and replenishing every three
your blood in its tree of vessels. Cell by
cell, in a year or so your liver lives
and dies. In eight, fresh fat reupholsters
flesh and in twice that span your bony
frame depletes and resurrects.

If you live to fourscore years or more
whatever wisdom you have earned, your
brain will be, more or less, the same grey
matter that was cradled in your yielding
skull at birth. You will hold in old ovaries (if
you have them) all the oocytes not germinated
menstruated, given away and your august
heart (unless you are one of many modern
miracles) will be hybrid—half the original
muscled organ, half of it grown new.

However long your life (unless you are one
of many modern miracles) the laminated
lenses you focus on this sight contain
the same crystalline slivers at their centre
which you first flexed to focus in the light.

Huddle

The whole world is this atheist's temple
and now I fear its death
but I am not ready to take up my shovel
to dig its grave, huddle
for small comfort like sheep
farewell the last birds.

Mud around the shrinking dam preserves birds'
footprints. They come to worship at this damp temple
alongside flocks of dusty sheep.
Some didn't make it. Death
caught them, they lie rotting behind the living huddle
and the dirt is dried too hard to shovel.

Firefighters wield hoses, shovel
firebreaks, smother outbreaks. Birds
fly ahead of the front, animals and people huddle.
They don't want to be burnt offerings at this temple
to placate the forces we've ignored, but death
can't be avoided. Farmers cry for their sheep.

So many carcasses of dessicated sheep
they bring in mechanical shovel
dig a pit to contain the death.
Before they bury them, the carrion birds
benefit, a small comfort. There is no temple
here for the grief-struck to huddle.

Heat and wind shift, a cold front. People huddle
into themselves, pull on jumpers made of sheep
or fibres drawn from plastic bottles. Thoughts, prayers from hilltop temple
are futile, and this southerly might shovel

new fuel onto the fire. The birds
are still, wait to see if this change means life or death.

We know it must come one day, death
but we can choose, in part, how soon and for who. Huddle
close, discuss how we will meet these times. Birds
depend on us, and bees, fish, people, trees, sheep
too. What will you do? Pick up your shovel
and suffrage to build tomb or temple?

A world without birds would be death
to the spirit, whether or not you subscribe to a temple. Come, huddle
as conspirators, not sheep. It's a builder's tool, this shovel.

Rakali

here am i   rakali   see me   if you are lucky   at the surface ...
i flick
white-tipped tail
submerge   ripples   disperse
my element water
  lithe droplet i
    flow
          sinuous
            wind
        to the
      bottom   through   cold layer
        current
            i am not cold
        i am warm fur bag of blood
    studded with silver
  blisters   air trapped under water's glove
one body   moving boneless   through another
porous like lake lined with slurry   earth mixed
with water   nothing is pure   i push snout
into mud   feel for water bugs   mussels   open up
eyes   ears   nostrils   skin   whiskers
every membrane   i am lake
sense this   whole   wet   volume   vibration
of particles   waves   i resonate
to echoes knocked back   fuzzy from sludge
sharp off rock   twitch
with mosquito larvae   rustle with carp
crash   with black swans landing
webbed feet braking   breaking liquid skin
a roo chased at dawn by dogs
    splashes in
        fills me with breathing

        heaving
muscular legs   turbulent
churning until   out   of   depth
exhausted   breathes water
        sinks

my forebears
    lived a winding
                    chain
            of
            pools
                streams,
        were stillness and running
    were hidden places
        their places
            shared with
                cod   smelt   frogs

hidden places
    still exist upstream   i forge that way
        cleave surface with snout   trail a rippling vee
    climb out   of water   out of myself
shake off
shake apart   smatter drops
on warm rock   preen pelt with teeth and tongue
sun teases moisture fur clumped
i steam
lift sinuous onto breeze

meet   my ancestors

we coalesce in cloud   look down at lake
they show me shape of water they knew
ropey flows laid over this bloated beast

only neck and tail
where river pours in
    and away
        match their memory

    we   fan   out   on   wind
fly   east to where the land lies like it did   before
the clearing   fencing   grazing   building   before
the changing   you dammed   nearly damned us
clotted the veins of this dry land   turned shallow
banks sheer   turned river to lake
made lake
a trap

you are skin bags of water too   propped up sloshing
on hard bones   will you atomise   one day
rise   look down with your
descendants?

ancestors' warmth evaporates
i cool   condense into saltless tears
rain into myself
flick white tail-tip   slip
back under lake skin
disappear

Special deal

a sidewise nod
a wink
the zoo keeper
in Antananarivo
beckons us

for a small gratuity
crumbled scruples
we can feed
the lemurs
honey

out the back
kindred fingers
a precocial human baby's
with soft spatulate palps
squeeze mine

turn them daintily
this way
and that
until I am licked
clean

Devonian roots in Cairo, New York

Scoured channels splay, could at a glance
be impression of sea stars, crinoids, clustered
mudworms, until you spot minute human
on the perimeter, remote controlling drone
for this bug's-eye view. Stamped in stone
three-hundred-eighty-five million years ago,
archaeopteris feet crept towards emergence
of seed. Shockingly modern roots radiate
guts-legs-feet in one organ stretched
to suck-grab-grip before flowers first unfurled.
Geoengineers, they crushed rock in super-slow-mo
bound the matrix, buttressed tipsy slopes, locked carbon
in cellulose, crocheted lacework of rootlets and fungus
for chemical conversation, vegetal flesh at death
turned to compost and coal. Green-furred forests
shambled many-legged across shifting continents.
Fortified the earth to accumulate life. Protected
fertile humus. Sheltered fragile humans. We—
so speedy, so industrious—have undone
much of their slow, quiet work.

Spontaneous generation

We believed in transmutation.
The wisdom of Aristotle, Anaxagoras. Pliny.
Seeds sprung from air, fleas from dust, maggots from meat.
Tapeworms from us, grubs given breath by the wind
or born of fire, we saw them crawl away from the flames.
We ate eels, though not earthworms, their juvenile phase.
Some say their germ is the corruption of age.
A recipe for mice, though we needed no more
wheat husks wrapped in soiled cloth.
For scorpions—basil, between two bricks, left in sunlight.
The sea left sweet gifts too, sand-seeded scallops
sea foam-spawned anchovies, oysters from algae.
Limpets and barnacles birthed from sea-wracked rock.
Some fledged into geese! With the seasons' turn
redstarts changed to robins, warblers to blackcaps
news came of crocodiles congealed from the far Nile's mud
swallows cased themselves in mud too, to endure winter
while swifts slept under ponds and streams, the unlucky
dragged up in nets, drowned as they woke.
Now we know the nerve sparks to move my hands
to type these lines before the impulse flashes in my mind
yet still we hunger for fresh wonders.

Five embalming jars of Dr Frederick Ruysch

Nature morte, closed system, no eco.
Pickled fish swims in your *liquor balsamicus*
noses the shallow dome at the base of the jar.
Above the air pocket at the vessel's neck
lid sprouts antlers of coral. Dead-eyed
piscine cousin perches there, angel
on a tombstone.

In the next jar, no visible meniscus. It is
filled with gases, correct element for this
pensive bird. Beak curved, glass eyes
downcast, claws cling to thorny buds.
Dead air trapped by a lid dense with
meadow flowers, a damselfly, mushrooms
all sucked dry of juice.

Its neighbour holds a foetal armadillo.
How it got from womb to jar I don't know.
Clearly this creature has never been born
translocated into vitreous sac, swimming
in new amniotic fluid. Unformed paws folded
empty sockets stare through the lid at
a tiny grassland it never explored.

A Surinam toad, babies still-birthed from her back.
Blisters erupt heads and legs. Was she in her
chemical bath when they hatched, or
plunged in mid-labour? Desiccated garter-snake
winds up the jar to a lid crusted with sponges
seashells. I am sure this mother of toads
never swam in salty water.

The final jar, a puzzle, ornate lid festooned
with branching coral resembling plastinated
veins. It takes seconds to recognise the contained
shapes—human child's forearm, with hand, skin
frilled around the severed end, decomposing into doily
nudging a hatchling turtle, wizened head
and fore-flippers bursting from ruptured egg.

Cryptic metaphor? Aesthetic composition? You filled jars
constructed dioramas like department store displays.
Infant skeletons decked with flower crowns dangle foetus puppets
from bare phalanges, cup blushing human hearts
weep into pocket handkerchiefs without monogram.
Were you doing death a service, making it seem sweeter?
Displaying your particular power over corruption?
Tsar Peter the Great visited your museum, kissed a mummy
bought the entire collection. Shocking in our hygienic now.

Forest burial

for Takayna

If I should die in Van Diemen's Land
lay me out in the forest, unadorned
near a fallen tree—so the stars can see.
Let the devils sniff my bones.

Let whiskers tickle my waxy skin
their pelts caress the shimmering dark
and finding I am made to eat
let the devils rend my flesh.

With gleaming teeth, bite into me
reveal my bright meat to the night
scrape the pink from ivory
growl and squeal my elegy
snap the tendons, lap the juice
cut my bones loose.

Let the devils scatter my bones
play with them like sticks and stones
break the predictability
of hip connected
to thigh
to knee.

Let the devils set me free.

Afterword

F-words is the result of my first six years of poetry writing. The styles and approaches across the poems are varied, as might be expected from a writer who is just starting to crawl out and explore the territory that can be poetry. This collection includes fiction, non-fiction, memoir and concrete poetry. Over these years, some lines of inquiry and interest have emerged.

I am a long-time lover of language, a 'word-glutton' as described in one of these poems. Poetry has given me a vehicle to pursue the translation and transformation of experience through language, and extend the possibilities of expression. Most valuably, poetry is a submersible vehicle, enabling me to dip below the surface of perception and rational analysis, sparking submarine connections and discoveries. A less linear mode of thinking.

Performance was my gateway into poetry, as a transfixed audience member and then as a performer. Much of my writing is intended for performance, but I have also come to appreciate the quieter possibilities of writing created for contemplation on the page.

I hope this collection offers the reader something of the theatrical outbursts, submarine expeditions and reflective contemplations that poetry has offered me as a listener, reader and writer.

Notes

Word Glutton: was shortlisted for the Axel Clark Poetry Prize 2015.

Wizard of Whitebridge: was previously published by *The Blue Nib* (online) on 31 May 2020 .

Honeybilla Moon Quartet: was previously published in the catalogue for exhibition 'Promised the Moon', ANU School of Art and Design Gallery, June 2019. According to "Eagle on the moon, The incredible space journey of Apollo 11" (Paul Hamlyn P/L, 1969, Australia), 'honeybilla' was the shorthand term adopted by the Apollo 11 astronauts in their radio communication, instead of the mouthful of 'Honeysuckle Creek-Tidbinbilla'.

Early: was previously published in Issue 3 of *Not Very Quiet*: *Women's Poetry Online Journal*.

The Patriarchs: was previously published in Issue 1 of *Not Very Quiet: Women's Online Poetry Journal*.

Disarming: was previously published in Issue 2 of *Not Very Quiet : Women's Online Poetry Journal*.

Häxan: is inspired by the silent film of the same name (which means 'Witches') directed by Benjamin Christensen in 1922. The film mixed documentary, drama and horror to explore the 'Malleus Maleficarum' in seven chapters. Versions with various soundtracks can be found on Youtube.

Gravity speaks to Joe Kittinger: tells the story of Joe Kittinger, a US military test pilot, and his final 'Excelsior' mission in 1960. In an effort to solve the problem of flat spin when pilots ejected at high altitude, he made a series of balloon flights and parachute jumps from heights only exceeded in 2012. Film footage from his missions and his own writing and interviews can be found online.

The Storm speaks to Eva Wisnierska: tells the story of Wisnierska's extraordinary survival after she was sucked up into a thunderstorm during a paragliding competition near Manilla, NSW, in 2007. Her story was made into the documentary 'Miracle in the Storm'.

If you: was previously published in *RABBIT 31: Science*, October 2020.

Huddle: was previously published as 'Sestina for Fire and Drought' by *The Blue Nib* (online) on 31 May 2020.

Rakali: Rakali is a recovered Aboriginal name for *hydromys chrysogaster,* called 'native water rat' by European settlers in Australia until recently. Rakali is the name from the Ngarrindjeri language, of people living on the Murray River, but has been adopted and promoted for common use. It is only one of many names for this animal around the Australian continent. This poem was created for 'LURK Burley Griffin', a series of poetry videos for the 2020 Contour 556 festival on the shores of Lake Burley Griffin, with Caren Florance, Melinda Smith and Zoe Anderson. All four videos can be found at: www.vimeo.com/channels/lurkburleygriffin

Devonian roots in Cairo: was previously published on 19 February 2020 by *Poets Reading the News*. It relates to the recent discovery of the world's oldest forests, as documented in the *Smithsonian Magazine* and *Current Biology.*

Five embalming jars of Dr Frederick Ruysch: This poem describes images from Frederic Ruysch's (1638-1731) *Thesaurus animalium primus* (1710) published in the *Public Domain Review.* It notes that Ruysch was a Dutch botanist and anatomist, remembered mainly for his groundbreaking methods of anatomical preservation and the creation of his carefully arranged scenes incorporating human body parts. The poem includes fragments from an essay by Luuc Kooijmans.

Acknowledgements

I first want to acknowledge the inimitable Candy Royalle, whose performance at the National Folk Festival in 2014 was my gateway to poetry. I know I am one of many who she inspired, motivated, taught and supported, and who mourn her passing.

I also want to acknowledge the generous, supportive, enthusiastic and diverse poetry community in Canberra and this region. Between the slams, open mics, readings, festivals and publications in this town, I couldn't have discovered poetry in a better environment. Once I start a list of individuals to whom I owe particular thanks for feedback, opportunities, support and advice, it is hard to know where to stop and I am afraid of omitting someone. But if I have thanked you before, I am talking about you now!

About the Author

Jacqui Malins is a performance poet, writer and multidisciplinary artist based in Canberra. She has performed at the Woodford Festival, National Folk Festival, Poetry on The Move and other events and festivals, and was an Australian Poetry Slam finalist in 2015. Jacqui created poetry shows "Words in Flight" and "Cavorting with Time" (with cellist Julia Horvath), which resulted in a chapbook of the same name (2018, Recent Work Press). Her work has been published *The Blue Nib, Not Very Quiet, Poets Reading the News* and *RABBIT.* Jacqui co-founded and organises Mother Tongue Multilingual Poetry events in Canberra.

Printed in Australia
Ingram Content Group Australia Pty Ltd
AUHW021154010824
397839AU00002B/15

9 780645 009019